# On the Way Up!

To Harriet,

I hope you enjoy
these few words.

Love
Little Donna !!

2006

# On the Way Up!

Anthology of Poetry

Donna L. Murrell-Murray

**VANTAGE PRESS**
New York

Published by Vantage Press, Inc.
419 Park Ave. South, New York, NY 10016

Manufactured in the United States of America
ISBN: 0-533-15247-X

Library of Congress Catalog Card No.: 2005904504

0 9 8 7 6 5 4 3 2 1

I dedicate this book to my God, my family,
and my many friends

# Contents

## Part II: Up a Little Higher!

# Preface

I am inspired by God's grace at this time and in this place. All I write is from his delight, given to me purely by inspiration. I take no credit for any of these works, they were all inspirationally given to me by God. All credit is due the one who gives the words and makes the way for me each and every day. All praise and thanks goes to my Lord and Savior, Jesus the Christ.

I am humble and eternally grateful to my Lord. I dedicate this poetry to my God, my family and all my friends. Special thanks goes to Ricole Juniel, who knows her craft so well, thanks Rikki. My prayer is that this poetry sends a positive message that is received as it is intended, to be uplifting. I hope all who read these few words understand where they stand. May God richly bless you.

ON THE WAY UP!

# On the Way Up!

# Part I

# On the
# Way Up!

# Purpose

The Ebb tide, a morning ride,
afternoon's glide,
the sun's rise.

A sweet surprise, life denies,
Seldom said good-byes,
All those whys.

For what purpose?
Do we rise, do we fall,
do we care, do we share?

Human shells so frail, purpose to entail,
whose news, what's blues, do we cruise?

Babies blessed, life then death,
no regret, all is sweat.

For what purpose?
Are we up, are we down,
are we clear, are we sound?

Seek love, peace, and joy,
is it to be found, before we meet the ground?

Life's best guest, is surely after death,
on Purpose, I guess.

# Almond Eyes

Opened wide those almond eyes,
brightly sprinkled with a twinkle,
eager to behold what this world holds.

Part of the human vine, quite sublime,
Aspire to a Rainbow.

Teddy bears add sparkle to her hair,
almond-eyed, sweet surprise,
so precious is the shine, of clear little almond eyes.

God lends his favor, to little chocolate dolls,
he dispels the night, with gentle morning light.

Sweetness, blessed with uniqueness,
wrapped up in chocolate spice,
so very nice, not full of ice,
shine beautiful almond eyes.

How great the fears, that hope the tears,
through life's years,
be just a few.

She needs the friend, who stays within, to hold the
        shine,
through any dark time.

Hope the seeds been planted true,
for, if we don't try,
how will she try, to reach the sky?

God's favor, certainly gives flavor,
to little almond-eyed, chocolate dolls.

Just remember, Candies from Strangers,
produces life's dangers.

# Aspire to a Rainbow

Aspire to a Rainbow,
'twas given as a sign, you know.

Written by the hand of God,
to let you know his way to go.

Aspire to a Rainbow,
'tis Heaven's Gate, you know.

Aspire to a Rainbow,
to the World God's love it shows.

Thank you God, for such a light show,
Aspire to a Rainbow, 'tis Jesus Christ, also.

Aspire to a Rainbow, true wealth it holds.
Aspire to a Rainbow, during creative hours,
after midnight,
yet, before you shower.

Aspire to a Rainbow,
pink, purple, yellow, blue and green.

Pink, a winter sunset, Purple, love a-glow,
Yellow, a summer minuet, Blue, sky, and
Green,—some grass grows.

Aspire to a Rainbow,
'tis Heaven's Gate, you know.

Aspire to a Rainbow,
Peace, is the after glow.

Aspire to a Rainbow,
God's love you will show.

Thank you God for such a light show.
'tis peace to seek, Heaven's Gate.

Aspire to a Rainbow, love will let you know,
find peace below, by the love you show.

As you Are inspired by a Rainbow.

# Beneath

Beneath God's hand is silk and sand,
Beneath God's hand, a mellow land,
Beneath God's hand is fellow man.

Beneath God's hand with patience stand.

If peace and love we do seek,
softly to each other speak.

Respect the life, cease from strife.
Kindred care for all who share.

Human-kind lost IN time, or
Human-kind lost THIS time.

# Calling

Who's calling, is it appalling?

So many people, in God's steeple.
I come with fears, rooted in tears.

Invest the stress, stand the test,
He'll do the rest, just give your best.

Press toward the mark, it is the spark.
Yours to embark, seek the ark.

Relief's in knowing, God is showing,
where you're going.

Don't let fears, bring forth tears,
remain stable, if you're able.

Yes, I'm calling, it's not appalling.
He who is calling, will keep you from falling.

Doors opened wide, take the strides, win the prize.
Take the chance, life enhanced, at a glance.

Press on and prance, this is your chance,
step out and dance.

Love's in growing.
Relief's in knowing, where you are going.

Take the chance, it's just a glance,
go ahead and dance.

# Consuming Fire

God is higher, should be desired,
he is a consuming fire.
Do you know him, poems can show him.

I have a reservation, to leave this station.
The ticket is free, you can come with me.

God is real, life's such a deal,
but you can't steal, what's his will.
He keeps the ledgers, silently measures,
all the pleasures.

When your pleasures are measured, will you find
        treasures?
Whose attuned, to what swiftly looms?
Fire consumes!
Desire a right, shed some light,
do what's right, before it's night.
Tried by fire, to test a liar.
Consuming fire, will take us higher.

## Content

Be content,
on distant shores, there is no more,
than what is here at your door.

Be real,
at times stand still, surfs of life, come from strife.

All pay a price,
who was right, who was wrong?
Does it matter after all?

Cling to love, listen to the songs of doves.
Peace is right, spells a good life.

Observe the word, it can be heard,
don't quench your spirit,
reverence in fear, for he is near.

Stand in love's garden,
seek your pardon.
Don't be hardened.

# Cracked Cistern

Who is the one, who takes time,
to talk a while, give that special smile.
One of God's designs—you or me?

We're all like a cracked cistern,
once we've ventured into life, broken by strife,
just part of life.
Our hearts can be spared, by the love we've shared.

How can a cracked cistern hold water?
It can't.

Plaster or glue, sometimes won't hold true.

How can a cracked, parched soul be refreshed?
Mercy and grace, will leave not a trace,
of sins erased.

Words from the Lord, are right—full of truth.
God fashioned your heart!
His words do impart, good news,
to plaster and mend our broken pieces.

In God's favor is sweetness and life.

Do you ever wonder, about the thunder?
If we could be free to really see, what would you look
for?
I ponder the sea shores.

Wonder where God stores the depths, and much more.

Cracked cisterns, be no more,
God is not afar off, on some distant shore.
He is not even next door.

Invite him in, he'll live within, there to mend.

## Dust

Déjà vu, illuminate a plume.
We've been in this room.
Seems a cartoon, sitting in a board room.
Big round table, made of maple.

How the dust looms, placating gloom.
Pride in full bloom, others to consume.

Lunch is at noon, won't forget to groom.
Consider the doom,
did we land on the moon?

See difference in a groom, when he jumps the broom.
Elevate your mind, you can't save time.
Consider a rhyme, drink from the vine.
get away from the Grind.

Great gust, chief dust, it's just us.
What fluff, makes up life's stuff.

Reflections in the mirror, disguise a hero.
What ever happened to Nero?

## Endangered

Life is yours, for a while, give a smile.
Big and small, God's got us all.

Step up higher, life's a mire,
God's a consuming fire.

We're in his hand, he lets us stand.
Oh, brilliant man, what's the plan?

Another's shoes, continue the blues.

Life all around us, we're not teachers,
we're just creatures.

We fear a bug, and miss a hug,
study a slug.

What's the plan, it's not your land.
You just stand, amidst God's plan.

Evolution stems from pollution,
there's no solution.

You can't save, it's God who gave.
Who's the slave, in this maze?

Stages and ages, continue life's pages.
Look around you, it will astound you.

It's not the stranger, who's endangered.

# Friend

Friendship, here and there,
help repair, the awful tear of despair.

We will remember,
if you tender,
some great splendor.

We're not owners,
of great moments.
There's a lender, we're just pretenders.

We play the games,
know the names, of all who came.
Just the same, where's the fame.

Trust the Spirit,
can't you hear it?
Is it far, that distant star?

Once alive, to my surprises,
we surrender, and blind our eyes.

Look within, to find the grin.
Pain or gain, meek or vain,
each bares a stain.

Life's a choice, choose to live it,
then, rejoice with clear voice.

Call his name, hear sweet refrains,
he's still the same.

Things great and small, are lent to us all,
a this, or that, a tit for tat!

I'm still a stranger, yet not in danger,
Love's my ranger.

# Giggles in a Dream

Giggles in a dream, are they so different from
wiggles up stream?

Who creates your dreams, or are they screams?

How precious to behold, as each miracle unfolds.
What's life about?
Some special shout?

Stretch out your hands, to understand,
you're just a man.

Breath in the air, dare to share,
look at the sand,
hold it in your hand.

Who's the man, who fished the land,
left his life, within our hands?

There's a place so special;
    the doors a flood, of God's own blood,
    the ways a gate, to God's Holy Spirit,
    take's no sense, to know to fear him.

Ponder a simple smile, linger a little while,
contemplate God's sweet relief,
with true belief.

Without the air, none can share.

Each day I'll write, from his delight,
God's gracious plan, throughout the land.

He gave the fish, you made the dish.
Why do we starve, it's not his wish.

Extend your arms, remove some harm.
Receive a smile, give one back.
Don't be so weak, you do not seek.

A hurtful man can't heal the land.

# Good Morning

Sit'n and think'n.
In the morning all is fresh,
a brand new page, from which to gauge,
all this rage.

The morning sets the stage,
for the next page of our lives.
In the morning, Sit'n and think'n.
Why do you suppose, we do impose?

Sirens scream'n, what's the mean'n.
Children play'n , laugh'n, cry'n, old folks are sigh'n,
some a die'n, stop that lie'n, must keep try'n.

Watch what you're buy'n.

If you're mean, can't fulfill a dream.
Anger unmanaged hides a savage.
If we could be, what we see, oh how happy we would be?

It seems so sad, and quite too bad,
that we can't have, and just be glad.

Thank God for the past, it spells today,
its not sad, what you've had.

In the morning the course is forming,
content to a purpose, life does surface.

Through God's grace, we still walk this place.
How can we explain,
what words can make plain, the reality we gain.

Sit'n and think'n.
Why do you suppose, we do impose?

Life is arduous deal with patience,
why do YOU suppose, we do impose?
Sit'n and think'n.
Have a GOOD MORNING.

# Grand Lady

Hair of whitening gray.
Skin gracefully sagging.
Limbs noticeably dragging.

Aching and shaking,
dependent and shy,
her toughness has faded.

Her mind comes and goes,
with thought of days past,
how long will she last?

Memories now dim, hardly ever a smile,
no interest in news or paying dues.
She doesn't need shoes.

Her husband's long gone, for many a dawn.
She clutches his memory with pictures and tears,
wondering why he left her here.

Death stands so near her,
Angels, surely they hear her coming.
They'll welcome and cheer her.

All her sisters, brothers, near kin and friends,
have already gone, how she holds on,
to each new dawn.

Failing muscles, weakened vessels embarrass her.
Embarrassment and shame seems the most that
    remains,
they taunt her small frame.

She sang life's song,
it's time she moves on.
Heaven bound, her new home will be sound.
Christ Jesus will greet her, and surely complete her.
Good-bye dear lady,

Sweet love song,
Grandma's gone.

## I Ain't Mad at You

I can't be mad at you,
that would hurt me too.

I ain't mad at you,
I'd need to be perfect too.

Truth and devotion, kindness in motion,
I ain't mad at you,
Can't we be glad instead of sad.

I ain't mad at you,
we just had to choose.

Laughter reins supreme.
Sadness shatters our dreams.
My heart longs to know from whence the water flows.

I ain't mad at you,
Hope is free, just look and see.

I ain't mad at you.

# Love

Hopes not gone, it rights a wrong.
Love's a song, sing it well.

Love's lots of fun, pace the run,
feel the sun.

Love can bloom in a sick room,
Don't look for gloom, see the moon,
it's beautiful in June.

Choose wisely, life's surprising,
don't miss the sun's rising.

Hyacinth, ginger mints,
sweet the scent that's Heaven sent.

# Mister

Mister, mister, my little mister,
loves his sister,
saw when he kissed her.

Mister, mister, hear when I whisper,
life can blister, or
it may be bliss sir.

Mister, mister, my little mister,
love your mother,
help your brother.

Mister, mister, my little mister,
loves the cover,
under which to hover.

Mister, mister, my little mister,
life has twisters.
Read the scriptures.

Live a good life, run from strife.
Seek the Christ.

Pray and pray, while you may,
lessens the price, you pay.

Be a good father, flee the sin,
that hides within.

Mister, mister, my little mister,
listen with your heart.
You'll find the part you play.

# None to Speak Of

Any good news?
Whose got the blues?
Got a pair of shoes?

None to speak of.

Showers in the desert,
Magic in a candle, too hot to handle.
Dreams in sun beams,
speeches for a queen.

None to speak of.

Blisters in the forest,
hope for the poorest.
Treasures which spare us.

None to speak of.

Deaths without lives.
Cries without whys.
Pain without lies.

None to speak of.

Goodness and Mercy
Grace freely given,
showers from Heaven.

Too much to speak of. That's Love!

# Pain

Mother's pain, is it in her brain?
Enduring grace, helps to wane the pain.
She bares the strain better in the rain.

Where's the example, for him to sample.
She views his back,
fears the lack.

What does she use to fill his shoes?
Can any man lend a hand?

He needs to stand, as a man.
How does she teach him?
With what to reach him.

She just sighs, as he cries.

She's not glad, he's so sad.
Her son's mad, at his DAD!

She sees he needs his Dad,
just to touch him, teach him, reach him,
give him a stand to be a man.

Could it be Dad can't see?

She bares the strain better in the rain,
you see, its pain unrestrained.

Still there's hope,
the best example, for him to sample,
is more than ample.

'Tis Christ's example, she lets him sample.

## Perseverance

Spend a life, seeking right
then you'll see love's liberty.

Keeping free, take time to really see,
the Master's plan is well at hand.

Be firm, stand, hold to the Lord's hand,
this is the way to the promised land.

Give no place to wicked sin,
Jesus Christ can live within.

Fall asleep, grounded in belief,
what sweet relief.
Jesus on your mind, wake up right on time.

Perhaps— in the nick of time.

# Pollution Solution

Stop cutting and gutting,
constructing and smutting.

Mop up the oil,
revegetate the soil.

Take sweet counsel together,
educate to conserve.

Put here to tend, now we must mend.

Imagine the land, as GOD planned.
World lend your hands.

Consider the steps we take
mistakes we make.
God will intake the meek, if we do seek.

Our life is a tale that is told.
Our place on this planet has taken its toll.

Extinction, with no distinction.

# Reap

Shall we reap?
In times to come, what have we done?

Surely our lives, represent the heaps of our choices.
You won't die, if you don't lie!

Wisdom is the fear of God.
Get wisdom and be wise, glimpse your life,
you can rise.

To refresh your soul,
to make you whole,
you can't be too bold, you will wax old.

Get wisdom.
Knowledge of right and wrong,
is surely not a song.

The choices we make, mold us, and hold us accountable.
Get wisdom, seek God.
He is in charge after all.

No matter how great your rise, or your fall,
you will answer some day for all.

Get wisdom!

# Remember

Walk in peace, remember with love,
all is sent, from Heaven above.

Remember a friend,
you may see him again.

Remember a child with a smile,
talk for a while.
Remember when, you were him.

Life's sublime, yours and mine.
Clock's keep time, who regulates your mind?

Keep it clean, be meek, not mean.
Someone's watching, what you're doin',
Surely seeing, what's a brewin'.

# Self-Reflection

All tired and weary, God is near thee.
Shakespeare penned a world of sin,
none can win unless God is within.

Help a child imagine in clouds.

Visualize the life, killed by strife.
Seek a higher plain, to play life's game.
It's really a shame, not to self restrain.

Expose the sin, that lurks within,
face to face is the place, to begin.
Look in the mirror, take in the view.

What lives inside of you?

You can't fight what's out of sight.
Never speak before you think,
the words you say are here to stay.

We're not alone under God's throne,
No need to moan.

A Bible verse, well rehearsed,
can sustain a empty purse.

Self is good when understood,
Self alone is on its own.

## Silent Good-bye

Where's the creature, starring in this feature?
My big strong man, where will you land?

Chief among dust, who do you trust?
Perhaps your lust?

Recognize the dust,
it's really a must, you see it's us.

I gave you trust,
dipped in your lust.
Stood by your side, how I tried.

Elevated, so elated,
self-invaded, really not shaded.

Yes, I'm jaded, 'cause
you invaded.

You stepped aside,
then you lied.
I watched our love, as it died.

As you faded, I knew we'd made it,
to where lost love is contemplated.

No Good-bye,
you just stepped outside.
Rings attached, keys to the latch.

Farewell my love,
all is done, enjoy the sun,
while you run.

Love's undone.

# Sing, Sweet Thing, Sing

Melodies ring, as you sing,
sweet thing, sing.

Pressures are real, as you sing,
suffer so much pain,
see no gain, sweet thing,
Sing.

Sounds of sin, tempts from within,
you have no gems, give them hymns.

Life makes you mean,
when you don't sing, sweet thing,
Sing.

No place to run, you'll miss the fun,
Clouds mist the sun.

Just sing, sweet thing,
let melodies ring, as you sing sweet thing,
Sing.

No one passes this way alone,
yet, still you moan.

Such a friend, to be let in,
Sing sweet thing, sing until the end.

## Strides of Life

All we have, is all we need,
from Christ it flows, abundantly.

We come along, sing life's song,
soon we're gone.

Where do memories go?
I don't know.

We try to meet you, that's why we seek you.
You walk alone, from dusk till dawn,
we need to greet you, and try to reach you.

Inspire our desire. We're afraid of the mire,
it's filled with fire.

We feel the breeze,
reflect on needs.

Take our rest,
through him we're blessed.

Life's crucial test, at grave side rests.
At the water's edge, noon rip tide collides,
life's strides are in good-byes.

Deep inside, patience lies, rightful strides is the prize.

Temperance and faith, win this race,
add love's grace,
stay life's pace.

# Take the Time

Help him to be what love can see,
You and he, is what made we.

Respect the brother, he'll be your lover,
Respect yourself, and his grace you will be.

Crown his head, instead of his bed.
Dress yourself in pride, he'll stand aside,
and watch your stride.

Be his bride, heal his pride.

You will discover, the man is your brother,
not only a lover.

Life goes much deeper, than the grim reaper.

Take your time,
sing your rhyme.
Hold his hand.

Don't give your treasures, simply as pleasures.
If you measure, the size of his mind,
lift up his head from your behind.

Just elevate your mind, take your time.
Watch the Son shine.

Be his treasure, he will measure up to the test.
You will see him at his best.
Pass his test, respect yourself.

God is in first place, he made the rules,
don't be tempted to be exempted.

Single Woman stay dressed, God can bless you with the
    best.
Respect each other, you will discover,
under the lover lies your brother.

## The Water's Eye

Lullaby, don't ask why.
Walk in the rain, ain't no shame,
nicely hides eyes, while they cry.

Meet the Water's Eye!

Drop a pebble into a stream,
see the rippled rings.

Feel the sigh, glaze the eye.
See a cloud as it swells.
What do you think? Can't take a drink,
from the Water's Eye.

Like ripples up stream, cling to your dreams,
matters not how remote they seem.

Don't lose the beam, life's real it seems.
In the Water's Eye.

Can't stop a ripple, it never comes back.
So is your life, you can't retrieve it,
you just leave it.

What will you leave?
Hopes for tomorrow, or some sad sorrow.

Am I alone, in my reality?
Is it just me?

NO!

# Today

Today is all that matters,
in the realm of reality.
Yesterday has departed,
tomorrow has not yet dawned.

Your walk, your talk, your smile,
loose any guile.

Like the coupling of a train track,
look, from left to right,
choose the path that leads to life,
seek after right.

A fresh new day, not marred in anyway.
Think about what you say.
Just today.

Sail toward God, his harbor is in love.
Be thankful you have been given, one more day.
Just today.

Our days are numbered,
the number of which only God knows.

All we have, that we can feel, even our needs,
that seem so real, are all enclosed in today.

Give praise and be thankful for,
Just Today.

# Tookie

Life is simple,
reflect on a dimple.

See trees, hear whispers through breeze.
In your heart's a fresh start.

Sing God's praise, feel the sun's rays.
Take someone's hand,
help heal the land.

Love not hate, is your escape.

Sinful man don't exploit the land,
It's in your hand, that was God's plan.

It's not too late, share the weight,
open love's flood gate.
Don't be late, time won't wait.

In much chatter, feelings can splatter.
Down through each age,
there's so much rage.

Does it matter, all that clatter?

Oh man, understand, there's peace at hand,
Only in a God-filled land.

# Twenty-four Hours

Twenty-four hours, mark each day.
Children play, mother's usually stay.
Will daddy go away?

Each moment of time you've spent,
truly is lent from above.
People we meet, they come and go,

Some stay a while, and make us smile.

Run in the sun, have some fun,
'cause when you're done, you're done,
no place to run.

Make some wishes, participate in your dreams,
life is so short, or so it seems!
Make someone happy, not just yourself.

Take pleasures in sharing,
with others who are caring!

Smell the flowers, walk in showers,
spend your hours as you please,
because spend them you shall.

You can't save the time God gave,
try not to squander, sometimes just wander.
Ponder a while, live in your style.

Just remember, you must tender,
an account of your splendor, to the lender.

Of each twenty-four hours.

# We

While we sleep, others creep.
The cool of morning, so rewarding,
moon light dimming, sun light shimmering.

There is a nook, where lingers a brook.
There is a haven, where hides a Raven.
What's man cravin'?
Is he worth savin'?

Why tempt God's hand, just understand,
this is God's land, we're mere man.

You and me, how could we be?
What if you're wrong, when days are gone?
Man's not dutiful, God's still beautiful.
Is there more, on some distant Shore?
How can he teach you, when he can't reach you?

Sons and maidens add to your days,
examine your ways.

Dare to seek him.
Perhaps he'll keep you.

# Wedding

Went to a Wedding,
Wondered where they're heading?

Down memory lane, into life sharing;
a sweet kiss, perhaps new born bliss.

Will they make it, or want to shake it?
Don't mistake it,
Life can break it.

Too much money, so little honey.
Wife's wearing white, groom's not uptight.

Friends and family all sharing,
songs to sing, rings, and things.

Cute young women, slim and trim.
All the young men so gentle then.

Wish them well, only time will tell,
where they're heading,
from this wedding.

Through life's refrain,
they'll surely change,

Hope little strain, this love thing.
As they're headed down memory lane.

Hour after hour, they'll need God's power.

# Words

We can be lonely, within us only,
but with words, we can be heard.

Words make you cry.
Words hide pride deep inside.

Words can encourage.
Words can discourage.
Words can prick just like a stick.

Words mistake, and forsake.
Words placate, and spit forth hate.

Words can share, and spare.
Words show care in despair.

Words deceive those in need.
Words compel, and cast a spell.
Words dispel, oh so well.

Words can tender the splendor we remember.

Words precociously mislead and feed on greed.
Words make good deeds.

Words guide the mind's eye.
Words paint a picture, still we can't see a melody.

Words can't be rescinded, once you've ended.
So when you speak, remember the meek,
You'll be unique!

## Your Man

Put down your man?
Your Son, does he understand?

Yes, he's a man, another one, perhaps your little one.

Mothers seize the lightning, is it frightening?
Is it your son, from whence you run?

Rolling thunder, makes me wonder,
whose hand we're under.

Help him to be, what will please,
Put down your man, he started God's plan.

Your man, formed by God's hand, help him stand,
he is your man, he named the sand.

MAN be a Man, for your SON, respect his Mom,
she's your brother's sister, mister.

Whistling winds, reel us in,
where we begin, is where we'll end,
if we remain rooted in sin.

There is a destroyer, think maybe it's he?
Can it be, it started with Eve?
Maybe you, maybe me, or perhaps it's we!

Woman, don't put down your man.

Your man is free, he should be household head,
the man's not dead, his respect's in shreds.

Love the lad, respect his Dad.
Can't you see, he is part of "Thee."

Help turn the tide, give back his pride.
Don't be deceived, we both need, each other, OR
we'll look around, and WE won't be.

What will your Son be? he is a man you see.
Help him keep free. Hug the brother, he loves his
    mother.

Help him to see YOU graciously.

# Part II

# Up a Little Higher!

# Introduction to Part II

By God's grace I'm still in this race, hoping to take first place. God is still inspiring me to take his poetry a little higher! To do his will is my desire.

My goal is to reach some individuals whom preachers may never reach, and to inspire those who already know the Lord, using Christian quietness. I wish to poetically imitate the parable of the cork.

The story goes; a cork suspended vertically by a silken thread, is put into motion to regularly strike a five-hundred pound steel bar suspended vertically by a chain. The minute cork not only causes vibrations soon after being put into motion by a slight push of a human hand, but also, after consistent regularity of time, causes the massive bar to swing like the pendulum of a clock.

By gently swinging the ideals of righteousness in spiritual poetry, against the steel bar of sin, I wish to tap at the collective human heart with poetic phrase. To matter in this life is important to me. I want to be part of the cause of righteousness, swinging like the proverbial pendulum across the hearts of human kind.

Most of all, as usual, all praise and thanks to Jesus Christ my Lord and Savior. My sincere thanks also to my family, friends, and now to my Representative, who have all helped me take another step higher. Thank you.

To you my precious recipients, I present for your continued reading enjoyment Part II: "Up a Little Higher!"

# Awaken

Awaken, be shaken.
old sinner man,
The Lord is at hand.

You've corrupted the land.
God understands,
it's part of his plan.

You can't rejuvenate, nor revegetate,
It is your fate.
Perhaps it's not too late,
to get things straight.

Heaven's gates are opening,
God's Messengers are voyaging.

Awaken, it's not too late.
If you get yourself straight,
can't tempt the hands of fate.

Wisdom and love will bless you from above.
Resound, resound, in love abound.
Cultivate your relationship with God.

The name of the Lord is important,
his name is love, patience, provider, peace, hope,
healer, guider, all in all.

Recover your testimony,
to the Glory of God.
We are blessed, he wants our best.

# Beautiful

Am I beautiful, when I rise?
Yes, because I am still alive.

The task last night,
has not been to create a
new grave site.

Are we beautiful, when we rise?
Yes, because we are yet alive.
One more morning, yes, another dawning, we are
    beautiful,
when we rise,
because last night we could have died.

We will be beautiful, all day,
because we have another opportunity
to be, or remain, saved.

God has given us another chance,
toward him to glance.
We are all beautiful when we rise, and
find, we are yet alive,
and able to rise.

# Cares of This World

The cares of this world,
can cumber and tear.

The cares of this world,
your heart cannot share.

The cares of this world,
are full of toil and snares.

The cares of this world,
can cause reparable breaches, but,
only God reaches those breaches.

The cares of this world, impasses create,
that close God's open gate,
if evil we mistake as fate.

Don't worry, don't hate, just wait, you will escape,
the cares of this world.
The question is,
in what state?

# Dewdrops and Raindrops

Did you know,
Little people in little places,
still leave great traces.

Quiet Service is never unnoticed,
God's eyes, span space and time.
They'll always find,
Little people in little places,
leaving great traces.

From God's glean none can hide, it seems.
His hand is on streams,
and in a child's dreams.

Thunderstorms and Dewdrops,
fill the same purpose.
Dewdrops reflect small spots.

A day of small things,
is still encompassed in all things.
All things, receipts, deeds, and pleas,
are always seen.

Dewdrops and raindrops still give water.
Snowflakes and earthquakes speak equally eloquently.

Listen!

# Doll

If you love me, can I get a minute?
If you love me, how long is eternity?

If you love me, do you have what I need?
All it takes is mutual respect.

If you love me, will you wait and see?
What I do in spite of me.
If you love me, speak truthfully.

If you love me, we can simply let it be.

After all you call me Doll!

# Favor

Awesome favor shall surround you.
God will always astound you.
If you trust him, he will ground you.

You will be better than,
when he found you.

Has God given you a vision or a dream?
Though impossible it may seem,
it's always safe to live in his grace.

Jump quickly on his command,
he holds your hand.
With God you can stand, on sinking sand.

Serve him in Awe,
reverence and respect, God's authority,
genius and great beauty.

Awesome is our God.
He is inspiring with dread,
without him, though alive, you are dead.

# Growing Old

What is depression?
Is it more than self compression?

It's your heart,
in recession or a fear of confession.

It's self alone,
with not even a moan.

You have grown.

How do we stand alone,
once we're grown?

An art or a craft,
what makes you laugh?

You're not at your best,
when life is in sunset.

What to do,
when you're too old to be young,
and too young to be old?

The world is cold, as you grow old.

Can you step out of the mold?
When you've forever been told,
it's sad to grow old.

# Help

A presence appeared alleviating fear.
Ever cried out when in doubt?

Remember a time, you didn't have a dime or even the
time?
Deep in your heart you know who took part.

Can you name him? Why don't you claim him?
Do we shame him?

It's really a shame, yet he still remains.
He will depart without your heart, can you afford that
part?

How will you feel, if you embark, forever in the dark?

Better think of the Ark.
God will not forever knock, while you say no.
Do you really want him to go?

You really should know, 'cause if he leaves,
where will you go, on unbent knees.
Who will hear your pleas?

# Inner Voice

What does he say?
When do you hear him?
None can compare, to the inner voice of peace.

It's the Spirit, can you really hear him.
Do you try or do you lie?

Are you sure you hear?
If you really hear, do you dare not to fear?

Do you answer?
Do you listen?
Are you afraid of what he has to say?
Does he chide you, does he guide you,
is it his spirit, do you fear it.
Are you sure you hear it?

Or is your inner peace, your inner voice,
there is a choice, sometimes it's not his voice.

How do you know, is it really his Spirit?
Do you hear it and still not fear it?

# Life's Longevity

On a distant shore, there is so much more.
The only way to permeate that precious gate,
is to understand and accept the Lamb.

Long life seems a curse, because life is unrehearsed.
Long life is a blessing, places mortality
in the realm of reality.

An old man's mind is not on his purse,
it is firmly directed towards his hearse.

Long life urgently steers, one's heart through his own
          years.
Can he smile during his last mile?

A chance to reach life's ultimate aim,
long life tends to correct, redirect, as we reflect.
Heaven bent, many years already spent.
Only believe, use longevity as the opportunity
to know God.

The ultimate aim, is still the same.
Life's sweet refrain, to know God's name,
and call always upon the same.

# Moments After

The moments after, may be filled with laughter.
We don't need another disaster.
Life is special.
Love's not free, the price is time.

Is any man righteous?
Hardly.

But you see he died for me.
In love you find the flood, of his righteous blood.
Like a veil, the fountain flows,
covers so well, all the hidden sin that lies within.

Helps us to stay on track, guards our back,
fill the space that lacks.

Precious is the fountain—that flows from Calvary's
    Mountain,
containing a righteous cover,
takes the place of an ardent or adulterous lover.

# Neighbors

Neighbors can be joy, neighbors can destroy.
Neighbors can be uncaring, never sharing.

Into a property lines, not the beautiful vines.

Neighbors, be mindful the land is not yours.
Neither the life that you fill with stuff, then fence it in.

Neighbors live next door, neighbors are on every shore.

Neighbors know the way, but they too can't stay.

Don't slay your neighbors with slander,
or think yourself grander.

You are a neighbor, I am a neighbor.
All God's people are neighbors.

Love your neighbor, as you love yourself.
Bless not curse, this, is the command of the Lord.
Who is your neighbor?
Everyone.

# Once Delivered

Do we need?
Is our need greed?
What if you're freed?

Are you happy when you've been delivered?
Does your freedom make you shiver?
Perhaps your heart's aquiver.

Do your eyes run rivers, when you've been delivered.

Is your freedom glum, once it's begun, can you run?
You don't dare think of where you've been,
because that was all sin, back then.

What do you do?
Don't look back, it is the past.
Remember it's gone at last.

Yes we need, to do some deed,
once we've been freed, so we don't recede.
Once Delivered—remember the pillar,
of Salt.

# Pictures

Down memory lane, pictures in a frame,
they have no names,
family resemblance remains.

Such a shame, no one left to explain,
the sweet refrain, of pictures with no names.

Clothed in years past, all of these faces, have left no
    traces,
of all the embraces, such strong faces.

Still no names fit these frames,
so much should remain, perhaps their fame.

But it's lost—pictures in frames, that have no names.
All that remains are their faces,
we don't even know the places—empty spaces,
pictures in frames they have no names.

We keep them just the same, their history remains,
whether we know their names.
When we see our pictures, bearing their features,
we add the names to pictures in frames.

# Shady

Don't want no part of your play ground,
Shady!
Don't want to disturb your party,
Watch you laugh'n hardy.
Shady!
Somebody stole your heart, left you feeling sorry.
Don't want no part of your play ground,
Shady!

Don't want to disturb your party,
watch you die'n while you continue lie'n,
Shady!
You look good on the outside,
Shady!
Something other than love, has replaced your heart.

Don't want no part of your play ground,
Shady,
Price is too high to pay, Shady.
Evil is not the way, Shady!
Human animals can still be shady!
Whether you be man or lady.
Shady.

# Stumble

A little stumble, can make you humble.
We often mumble when we stumble.
Afraid of the dark?
Life's filled with sharks.

Humility can set you free if you want to be.
We stumble,
Because we can't see,
the stretched out hand from the Son of Man.
It is him who is calling.
His hand keeps us from falling.

No message today, turn life's page,
mourning will be turned to joy.

There is hope in the end.
Set your heart toward the high way,
don't stumble onto the bi-way.

Let every weary soul be satiated,
with the love of God Almighty.
Humility is a virtue.

# Tears Well Inside

When tears well inside, they come up through your
    sighs,
until they reach your eyes.

When tears well inside, we put pride aside,
and we just cry.

We cry unto the Spirit, to set us free.
Your heart is a moan, and your mind doth groan,
because you're alone.

Your nose seems to sting, when you release that thing.
Reflect on your dreams.
Reality seems, swiftly unclean.

Inhale your screams,
feel your needs, as tears well inside.

They dim your smile,
but just for a while.

# Temporary

Do we know, just how we grow?
Wish life weren't so cold.

Listen and do, you won't be blue forever.
Love your husband, while you can, life or death can
      make him leave you.

Love your children, realize they grow each day,
and then they too, go along their way.

Mom and Dad, they can't stay.
Grandma, Grandpa are in their grave.
Where there is a will, whose way?

Just today are we able to stay.
All things are temporary, seek a sanctuary.

God is real, and the only lasting phrase on life's stage.
GOD alone remains, at the end of the Day,
He alone will never go away.
Even at death, is he still yours.
All things are temporary,
EXCEPT, GOD.

# Trees

Would you pray for a tree?
Would you get down on your knees for a tree?
Would you cry and even sigh for a tree?

Yes, Lord.

The fragrance of a Lilac Tree,
refreshes the air as a mountain breeze.
The brilliance of a precious tree,
always points to God's glory.

The quiet sound of a budding tree, is gloriously
     everlasting.

The strength of God, is steadfastly represented
in every tree, down to its longevity.

The color of an Autumn tree is amber bright,
the leaves shine bright in the morning light.
Every tree is painted from red to green,
the blackening stem shows summer's end.

View a tree and you will see,
God is so mighty.
Simply look upon a beautiful tree.

Would you pray for a tree?
Yes, Lord.

For a tree is a gift from Thee.
Trees are God's legacy, planted here for all to see.

As you have prayed,
The Lord your God
Will save.

Believe it,
Receive it,
You can Achieve it.

Pray for a Tree.

# Two Things

Wisdom and Understanding.
Two Things,
Jealousy is the rage of man, God said.

Vanity can pause God's hand.
Two Things,

He that walks uprightly, walks surely.
A soft answer turns away wrath, God said.

Before honor is humility.
Two Things,

Man's goings are of the Lord.
How can a man, understand his own way?

Labor not to be rich.
Labor to go home,
for surely there is an end.

Wisdom and understanding,
Two Things—everyone needs.

# Watery Grave

God made Adam, God made Eve.
He breathed life, into you and me, from his eternity.

He sent his Son, to make us one with him.

Sin drove two stakes, through holy hands,
and through his feet to be complete.

For his head, sin wove a crown, from the thorns, his
    blood did run,
down to the ground, without a sound.

Sin drove a spear, through his side,
He hung his head and then he died.
To forgive this sin, He moved within.
To each heart, his death brings a fresh start.
Submission, immersion, earnest delight,
symbolizes the death of our idolness.
Let us come to the water, be baptized.
Beyond this life lies Heaven to gain, and
Hell to shun before you're done.

Come, be one. Come to the water, be baptized.

# Wisdom in Part

One whom would come running, into the admonition of
    the Lord,
is wise indeed. Wisdom in this life is truly your only
    need.

A rare jewel is Christ, a true love worth finding.
This mortality shall indeed, be clothed in immortality.
For every one life, there is surely one death.
The eyes cannot behold God.

The Lord has no form for he is Spirit.
Wisdom is the fear of him.
Wisdom is to hear him.
Wisdom is to draw near him.

Wisdom is knowing that little is much with Christ
    Jesus.
Set your heart to hear in part.

Wisdom is knowing one is righteous.
Clothe your prayers in his righteous blood, they'll be
    heard in Heaven above.

Wisdom is to live today, knowing the end will come.
Wisdom in full, is in God's will.
Desire a right you'll see the light.

# You

I don't know you.
Who are you?
Where are you from?
I don't want to run.

I don't know you.
What do you dream?

Out of thin air, you were there.
I don't know you.
Should I, could I, dare I,
do I,—want to?

I don't know you.
Are you the sweet dream you seem?

Did I see YOU,
when I met you?

Could you be just a dream?
Dare I be bold, I need to be told,
Yet,
I'm afraid of the cold.

Are you free to come and see?
You don't know me.
Should you, could you, dare you,
do you,—want to?

I lean on a wall here in this hall,
after all you are so tall.

But,
If you're not free,
It's no surprise to me.
We'll just let it be.

# You Can't

You can't.
You can't.
You can't!

You can't overpower God's force.
You can only work with the source.

Truly attempt remorse,
for your life of course.

A very complete experience is;
philosophy, theology, yourself, and
perhaps someone else.

The visual world is, shapes and patterns.
We think of Saturn.

You can't. You can't. You can't!

You just are.
So just be!

## Your Stuff

What belongs to you?
Maybe your shoes, or perhaps your own blues?

Who owns your feet? Perhaps some street?

Is there a hand on you? I really thought you knew.

He helps us too.

Do you change your heart?
You can't even start.

Afraid to touch you face to face,
with these words,
I do embrace you.

Your stuff,
just things.

Dust is all that will remain of the same.
Such a shame to base your fame,
on your stuff.

# Part III

# A Way
from the
Mire!

# Introduction to Part III

A Way from the Mire is another step higher. When we seek directions to a place we want to go, we need to know the names that will lead us there. Search the name, it remains the same and refers to the only One way.

If you read no further than the next two pages, I will have given you the map. I have done my best, now God will do the rest.

I now present to some, and introduce to others the name that IS:

A Way from the Mire!

# The Name

Jah—God
Elohim—The Creator,
Elyon—God Most High.
El-Roi—God Who Sees,
El-Shaddai—All Sufficient One.
Adonai—The Lord Master.
Jehovah—The Self Existent One.
Jehovah-Jireh—The Lord Will Provide.
Jehovah-Rapha—The Lord Who Heals.
Jehovah-Nissi—The Lord My Banner.
Jehovah-Shalom—The Lord Is Peace.

Jehovah-Sabaoth—The Lord Of Hosts.
Jehovah-Raah—The Lord Is My Shepherd.
Jehovah-Shammak—The Lord Is There!
Jehovah-Mekoddishkem—The Lord Sanctifies You!
Jehovah-Tsidkenu—The Lord Our Righteousness.

Jehovah-Ishi—[Hosea 2:16, KJV (not interpreted)].
El-Eelohe.
I AM That I AM.
Jesus The Christ. Holy Spirit.

## Farewell My Friends

Take hold of the Word of God.
Take it all the way to Heaven, and
it is a way from the mire.

Look toward your reward.

Look for and receive;

Supernatural outpouring of power.
Supernatural outpouring of portion.
Supernatural outpouring of passion.
Supernatural outpouring of purpose.

Listen to hear,

WELL DONE, GOOD AND FAITHFUL SERVANT.

You will do well in Deed!

Jesus is my Friend, please meet Him.

## Letter To God

Dear God, Jehovah, God of Abraham, Isaac and Jacob, God of King David, God of MINE:
Thank you for my calling.

Dear Lord:
Thank you God, for the gift of poetic phrase, for which I give you all the praise. I stand on your words, I've tried to observe. I receive what you give. Thank you for the way to live.

I thank you for each breath you so graciously give, that allows us all to live just one more day. I delight in you, and I receive the desires of my heart. Thank you God. You are more wonderful than my heart can imagine. Thank you God, for your words to observe. Thank you for loved ones, and friends, thank you for health and your Holy Spirit. I revere you in awe because you are God.

I thank you for all your children who pass my way, especially the ones you've loaned directly to me, my daughter, grandchildren, my mother, father, sisters, brothers, even lovers, grandmothers, grandfathers, aunts, uncles, cousins, and family in Christ. I thank you for the lives I may never meet or even greet. Thank you for the chance to live and learn, even to yearn.

We are all flowers in your garden, thank you Lord for your tender ways. Give me the strength to live each day under the Holy Blood that saves. Thank you most of all for just being GOD.

Amen.

Sincerely,
Your loving hand maiden,
Your willing servant,
Your forgiven lamb. Me.

# Part IV

# Melancholoy Poems of the Heart!

# Introduction to Part IV

I love poetic verse. It is my passion, my art form, and my contributions to my moments here on earth. I love poetic minstrels of which I am one. I am romantically reclusive, given my script purely by inspiration thanks to my God.

# Until Death Do You Part

To love a lifetime is a gift from God.
To live together until twilight is a coveted prize.
To see the splendor of each gender together,
is a lesson in living.

To have family and friends,
is an abundant Life.
To have and to hold, till death does part,
is Marriage, God's way!

# When God Comes

What will you be doing, who will you be wooing?
Perhaps you'll be suing. When God comes.

Where will you be, eating, drinking, making merry,
perhaps you'll be staring into a cloud,
Feeling quite proud. When God comes.

Who will you be with, someone else's husband or wife,
perhaps you'll be saving a life, helping out with all this
    strife!
When God comes.

Will you be walking, talking, stalking,
singing, swinging, stealing, so drunk you're reeling?
    When God comes.
Will you be wishing, hoping, praying. What will you be
    saying?
When God comes.
Will you be slumming, bumming, or perhaps you'll be
    humming.
When God comes.
He is coming! How, when and where will he find you?
When he breaks through?

# Can't We See One America?

Why can't we see, we're already free, especially in
  diversity.
Oppression, depression, recession,
where's the right to legislate plight, blight, or to not be
  polite.

I can't hear you, if I fear you, how do I come near you?
Respect me, I'll respect you, I believe we are
  government too.

How seldom we do appease, all the ones we've tried to
  please,
really, self's the only one that's eased.

Love comes in degrees, educate good among the masses
  of all the classes.
Thoughtful study, constructive dialogue positive action,
  value every person to
strengthen our shared foundation,

For One America.
Appreciate our differences, live toward human peace at
  home.
In One America.
Love's the solution, Don't just say it, DO it
For One America.

# Disposability

Are we disposable, are WE disposable?—disposability!
Human disposability, go mentally yonder, ponder,
wonder in life's disposability.

War—hate, late—great, confirm disposable state.
Organ use, reuse, misuse—disposability?
Furthermore, forevermore, or even more, repugnant
     redundancy.

Disposable flesh, some distinction at best, human,
animal, plant, liquid, solid—gaseous—Us? Hushed!
Yes,—forevermore!
Knowably, honorably, naturally, intentionally,
Whatever the relativity—cosmically, universally,
     disposable.

Disposable.
Rush to life that ends in death, rate of return
     Zero—Disposable.
Life is disposable, so—possibly enjoyable in spots.
Are we disposable poetically?
Great minds waste times, interjecting wines, from
     someone else's vine.
Think—about it!

# In the Moment

Live in the moment, live in the moment
until the moments increase or cease.

Momentarily, lingering, in the moment.
Sweet moment, uncomfortable moment, terrifying
      moment, grievous moment,
Longing moment,—loving in the moment.
Live each moment, send something forth like minstrels
      of verse, be touched by the
Universe.
The first moment—creates a memory,
Shared moments—history or mystery,
The last moment—ends a lifetime.
Live in the moment! For—the moment—you are,
      truly—in the moment.
Life is moments.
Live in each and every inevitable moment, delectable
      moment,
detestable moment, You do! conscious or not, live each
      moment.
Live consciously moment by moment.
Where are you now?
Precisely—in this moment—with me.
Love moments—they are all—you have—at the
      moment.

# Ironic Philosophy

Why do we adorn our lives with trinkets,
Fill our minds with useable knowledge?
Is all knowledge useable?
Whatever for?—Money

To multiply and act dignified—what pride.
Time frames, some shames.

Humm
Does a mirror talk too much?
Mine does, how about yours?

# Legacy

Speak to the millennium, in deep retrospect of the
    pendulum.
Environmental endangerment, human kind racing
    toward self-extinction,
with no distinction.

Examine your mind, educate the times,
the measure of a man cannot withstand the strands of
    his head,
nor the nurture of his bed, where he rests in shreds.

Engaged souls in monetary molds,
how bold, this recycled dust which is us!
On this land another will stand, maybe!

Trees converted into totem poles,
Blood still waters pot holes,
This life, so much strife, yet we love somebody, some
    soul.

Mankind arrives and departs just like the start,
Whose hand guides this land—not man's, Legacy.

## Measure Your Treasure

Friendship of forever, is the measure of love's twine for
    all time.
As friends unite on life's highway,
love twines you to each other like no other.

Marriage is the morning kiss of an angel,
that made the sun to blush, and the rush is called
    sunrise.

Measure your treasure, commingle each pleasure
    forever,
the result is love promised.

Your vows complete your true treasure,
as friends become one, life's love is only begun,
beside each other as long as time binds you.

May God embrace you in His grace,
as together you run this race at a true pace.

# Middle Age

Radiant at its best, Complexity complete.

Skin subtler now, With knowledge of care
Understanding, relished. No arrogant air.

Age in the middle
Can understand because, You care, by way of being
     there.

Just a touch conveys hello, life is mellow as a whole
In full bloom.
Culture among your own, are we all our own?

Can you sing and dance
Seek adventure and romance
Social conscious
Rage
Passivity
Social good—is it understood?

# Romance

The height of the emotions—expressed in poetry.

What shall I see
To tell thee of,

What shall I feel
In the instant reality.

## Shades of Blue

Blue color life,
Blue sky—mountains high, river runs,

What's already in life
When you meet that stranger?

Profoundly the earth moves,
Slightly under your feet! The Ocean in motion.

The haze surrounds him
As all other briefly take leave from your consciousness.

Felt on one side?
Oh how I wonder, as emotions thunder.

## Spending Time

As you reflect on time you spend,
You can reminisce on things that end,
However, the end is never then,
As once again you begin.

Scattered moments, pressed with
life's cargo—cargo—cargo,
let go. Peace is the after flow,
of cargo—let go.

Afraid to touch you face to face,
With these words, I do embrace.
Laughter runs supreme,
Sadness shatters dreams.

Think about what YOU say, just today,
As you begin again with the time you spend.

# Whatever Happens on Sunday

Whatever happens on Sunday, or Monday
Or any other day for that matter, it happens only once!
   Now.

Why then do we live it, over and over at will.
Because, now itself is our reality. I hope you see.
Mirrors talk too much?
If one is ask to say something, one must have something
to say, we hope, anyway, relative to who.

If one dares to speak, the magnitude to them, is
   tremendous,
one cannot bear nor promote, tremendous magnitude—
   alone,
for there is insufficient energy, maybe.

You know we think so much more of ourselves,
collectively, mutually, individually, and
conveniently. Or extremely conversely.
However, we are power or what
We are perceived to be . . . "Or Not to Be."

Whatever happens on Sunday, effects we,
Whether we is a man, woman, children,
Creatures of the wilderness, male, female and off
   springs.

Life happens on Sunday, Monday or any other day.
Affordable housing, for who.
Piles of plenty, in what pockets, poverty sockets
reorganized by the developer or was it someone's home.
Air pollution, ain't no solution.

Pain effect us, my pain, your pain, the pain of
A homeless baby, pain vicariously, empathetically
    sharing
The pain.

Fix it,
love the garden of people and kindred, do the right
    thing,
live harmoniously in your reality,
reflecting on all endangered species and
CHANGE!

# Woman Black

Not in spite of,
Not instead of,
With my Carmel, Hershey, cinnamon gold blackness,
I come,
Standing.
Queen lovely princess,
Black pearl skin,
I am, I can, I shall, I have accomplished
Womanhood's stark elegance.

Black woman,
Woman Black
Sugar Stacked.

Brown sugar, impressive lips—render the kiss,
With memorable bliss.